REPORTS FROM THE FRONT IN WWII

Paul Mason

Crabtree Publishing Company

www.crabtreebooks.com

Author: Paul Mason
Editor: Kathy Middleton
Production coordinator: Ken Wright
Prepress technician: Margaret Amy Salter
Series consultant: Gill Matthews

Picture Credits:
Corbis: Bettmann 17
Fotolia: Alexey Shadrin 13
Getty Images: William Vandivert/
    Life Magazine/Time & Life Pictures 24
Library of Congress: 5
National Archives and Records Administration: 4, 8, 10,
    16, 19, 20, 22, 23t, 27, 29l, U.S Navy/Conseil Régional
    de Basse-Normandie 21b
Rex Features: Roger-Viollet 25t, 25b, Sipa Press 18, 26
Shutterstock: Cover, Timothy R. Nichols 6l, 7
U.S. Navy: 14, Chief Photographer's Mate (CPHOM)
    Robert F. Sargent, U.S. Coast Guard 21t,
    Naval Historical Center 15t
Wikimedia Commons: 6r, 9, 12, 15b, 29r, National
    Archives and Records Administration 11, 28,
    U.S. Army Air Force 23b

Some of the quotes in this book are fictional and are designed to illustrate what it might have been like to experience the events recorded.

Library and Archives Canada Cataloguing in Publication

Mason, Paul, 1967-
    Reports from the front in WWII / Paul Mason.

(Crabtree connections)
Includes index.
ISBN 978-0-7787-9905-4 (bound).--ISBN 978-0-7787-9926-9 (pbk.)

    1. World War, 1939-1945--Juvenile literature.
I. Title. II. Series: Crabtree connections.

D743.7.M38 2011   j940.54   C2010-905302-8

Library of Congress Cataloging-in-Publication Data

Mason, Paul, 1967-
Reports fron the front in WWII / Paul Mason.
    p. cm. -- (Crabtree connections)
Includes index.
ISBN 978-0-7787-9926-9 (pbk. : alk. paper) -- ISBN 978-0-7787-9905-4
(reinforced library binding : alk. paper)
1. World War, 1939-1945--Juvenile literature. I. Title. II. Series.

D743.7.M363 2011
940.54--dc22

2010032441

Crabtree Publishing Company

www.crabtreebooks.com   1-800-387-7650
Copyright © 2011 **CRABTREE PUBLISHING COMPANY.**
All rights reserved. No part of this publication may be reproduced, stored in a retrieval system or be transmitted in any form or by any means, electronic, mechanical, photocopying, recording, or otherwise, without the prior written permission of Crabtree Publishing Company. Published in the United Kingdom in 2010 by A & C Black Publishers Ltd. The right of the author of this work has been asserted.

Printed in the U.S.A./082010/WO20101210

Published in Canada
Crabtree Publishing
616 Welland Ave.
St. Catharines, Ontario
L2M 5V6

Published in the United States
Crabtree Publishing
PMB 59051
350 Fifth Avenue, 59th Floor
New York, New York 10118

CONTENTS

POLAND INVADED!

Yesterday, Polish men, women, and children hid in terror as German tanks rolled past their doors. "The ground shook as the tanks went by," said one woman. "We hid in our **cellar** for 14 hours, with nothing to eat."

A German soldier throws a grenade at Polish forces.

Polish forces retreat

Poland's army is **retreating** from the border with Germany. "We are falling back to the east," reported a grim-faced Polish officer, "to places where we will be able to destroy their tanks. Then the Germans will have a hard fight on their hands. But we need help from other countries."

4

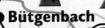

The German leader, Adolf Hitler, is responsible for the attacks on Poland.

BACKGROUND TO THE ATTACK

The attack has happened because the German leader, Adolf Hitler, claims that parts of western Poland belong to Germany. Many German speakers live in the area. Hitler says they want to be part of Germany, not Poland.

Help from abroad?

Polish leaders hope for help from Great Britain and France. The three countries are **Allies** and have joined forces to fight Germany.

The Allies have said Germany must not invade Poland. But it is not clear what else they can do to help since Germany lies between them and Poland.

JEWS TO BE SENT EAST

DATELINE
19 Oct 1939
GERMANY

There was widespread disbelief and horror among German Jews yesterday, as the **Nazi** government announced that Jews must pack up and leave the country.

JEWS FORBIDDEN

Polish Jews were the first to be rounded up by Nazis. Now the German Jews have met the same fate.

Horrified reactions

"My family has lived here for hundreds of years," said one Jewish shopkeeper, who did not want to be named. "I fought for Germany in the First World War. Why must I leave? This makes no sense."

Trains to the East

The government is arranging trains to take Jewish families to Poland. They are to live in **ghettos**—places where only Jews can live. Government forces will begin to round up Jewish families in the next few days.

Bütgenbach

Lunebach

Büllingen

NAZI GERMANY AND THE JEWS

The Nazis have taken many steps against the Jews since Hitler became leader in 1933:

- In 1933, Jews were banned from working as teachers and civil servants.

- From 1935, Jews were no longer allowed to be German **citizens.**

- From 1935, Jews were not allowed to marry non-Jewish Germans.

- On 9 November 1938, Nazi supporters spent the night smashing up Jewish businesses and **synagogues.**

The burned-out shell of a Jewish synagogue

Gouvy Burg-Reuland Habscheid

Troisvierges

PARIS FALLS!

DATELINE
15 June 1940
FRANCE

The German **conquest** of Europe continues. Last night news reached us that German forces have captured Paris. France now seems sure to surrender.

Hitler in front of Paris's famous Eiffel Tower

Allied forces scattered

Germany's fast attack left the Allied forces scattered. Over a million French soldiers were taken prisoner. Those not captured changed out of their uniforms and slowly made their way home. "It was chaos, utter chaos," one Frenchman told me. "The Germans just kept coming. It was completely hopeless."

Paris waits

In the French capital, people do not know what to expect. The markets are empty, and the streets are quiet except for the sound of German patrol tanks driving by.

Evacuation at Dunkirk in France

Some Allied soldiers were able to escape from France. Filthy and exhausted, they have been brought across the English Channel. "The boys fought their way out," reported Sergeant Major Harris of the British Guards Regiment. "And they've lived to fight another day. I'm very proud."

Exhausted soldiers during the battle for France

THE MIRACLE OF THE LITTLE SHIPS

With the Allies fast losing ground at Dunkirk, the emergency call went out to all civilians with any kind of vessel to come to the aid of the retreating troops. All kinds of boats—battleships, yachts, and lifeboats—brought more than 300,000 Allied troops back to England. This gave rise to the term "Dunkirk spirit," the nation pulling together in a crisis.

*From a radio broadcast on June 5

BLITZ ON LONDON!

DATELINE
30 Dec 1940
BRITAIN

Germany's bombing of **civilian** Londoners continued last night. Several streets in the East End were flattened. Survivors are still being pulled from the **rubble**.

Smoke drifts in front of the dome of St. Paul's Cathedral in London.

Early alerts

Shivering on the rooftops in the cold November air, the firewatchers knew the German bombers were coming. First the drone of their engines was heard, and then flashes of exploding bombs were seen in the East End. Another night of the Blitz on London had begun.

Firefighters joined by soldiers

As parts of the city burned, neighborhood firefighters leaped into action. Without their bravery, a church hall in Greenwich where hundreds of people were taking shelter would have burned down.

Londoners still go to work. The bombing has not dampened their spirits.

The firefighters were helped by soldiers at home on **leave**. "I come home for a weekend's rest!" said one **Tommy** with a soot-blackened face. "But you've got to fight Hitler wherever you can, haven't you?"

Spirits remain high

The bombing has not broken people's spirits. "Hitler can eat his hat for all I care," said Gladys Knight, standing in front of her bombed-out house. "Londoners will never give in."

WORDS FROM THE QUEEN

"I'm glad we've been bombed. It makes me feel I can look the East End in the face."

—on Buckingham Palace having been hit by bombs

LENINGRAD UNDER SIEGE!

DATELINE

9 Sept 1941

SOVIET UNION

The German Army yesterday surrounded the great Soviet city of Leningrad. Leningrad's heroic defenders are readying themselves for a long **siege**.

A Soviet fighter waits to take a shot at the enemy

Germans dig in

Germany's original plan to capture and destroy Leningrad has failed. Now, the Germans will try to starve the city into defeat. To the south, the German Army is preventing supplies from getting through. In the north, Germany is doing the same, with the help of the Finns.

Supplies running short

Leningrad's defenders are running low on food. Warehouses full of supplies have been bombed and destroyed by the Germans. There may only be enough left to feed people for four weeks. But the defense will not end—Leningrad's **munitions** factories will make sure that the city does not run out of guns or bullets.

SHOE SOUP

Civilians in Leningrad are already finding food hard to come by. But Russian resourcefulness knows no boundaries! The people have discovered that boiling up leather shoes for days makes a thin soup.

"It may not be very nice, but it beats starving to death," said Yelena Golunskaya, as she stood by her stove.

Surviving winter

The freezing weather will make survival harder for Leningrad's people. But Russians are used to snow—and when Lake Ladoga freezes over, supplies will be able to reach the city across the ice.

People wait for Lake Ladoga to freeze...

PEARL HARBOR ATTACKED!

DATELINE
8 Dec 1941
UNITED STATES

Destroyed battleships smolder next to docks or lie at the bottom of the ocean. Bodies of servicemen rest in their coffins. Yesterday, the horror of war came to American shores.

Smoke pours from destroyed battleships

Surprise attack

Japan's attack on the U.S. Navy base at Pearl Harbor took everyone by surprise. "At first we had no idea what was happening," one sailor reported. "The sky was suddenly full of planes. But when the bombs started to fall, we realized we were under attack."

The full extent of the damage is not yet clear. Reports suggest that eight battleships, three cruisers, and three destroyers have been damaged or wrecked. An estimated 2,402 people have been killed and 1,282 wounded.

Bütgenbach

Lunebach   Büllingen

The ships at Pearl Harbor were simply sitting ducks.

PRESIDENT DECLARES WAR

President Roosevelt has declared war on Japan. He announced that, "No matter how long it may take us...the American people in their righteous might will win through to absolute victory."

The **mobilization** of American forces is expected to begin immediately. Meanwhile, anti-aircraft guns are being set up on the beaches and hills of California in case of Japanese attacks.

Islanders terrified

On Hawaii, people are scared. Stories are being told of a Japanese invasion fleet nearing the islands. As far as is known, this is not true. But, as one Hawaiian homeowner said, "They didn't think the Japanese aircraft were sneaking up to attack us, either."

Japanese fighter planes line up to begin the attack.

JAPANESE TAKE MANILA

DATELINE
3 Jan 1942
PHILIPPINES

The American flag no longer flies over Manila. The Japanese yesterday captured the city. However, the determined U.S. and Philippines forces fight on.

Bodies all over

It has taken Japan's troops almost a month to reach Manila. "We made them pay in blood for every inch," one of the **Filipino** fighters told this reporter. "Our people will never stop fighting the invaders."

U.S. soldiers surrender to the Japanese in Manila.

Resistance continues

Filipino **resistance fighters** are still attacking the Japanese from their bases in the mountains. Meanwhile, U.S. forces are withdrawing to the Bataan **Peninsula**. The battle for Bataan is expected to be the fiercest of the war so far.

DISASTER AT DIEPPE

DATELINE
0 Aug 1942
FRANCE

A failed assault by the Allies ended in horrific loss of life yesterday. Nearly 1,000 Canadian soldiers were killed and 2,000 taken prisoner when the biggest-ever combined force landed on the beaches of Dieppe in France.

Over 6,000 troops, 5,000 of them Canadian took part in the mission.

Fiasco or valuable exercise?

Operation Jubilee, as the raid was called, is being criticized for having no clear mission and not providing ground troops with enough air and naval support. But senior military insist that, although the cost in lives was high, the lessons learned here will ensure the success of future Allied invasions.

NO HOPE

"For eight hours, under intense Nazi fire, I watched Canadian troops fight the blazing, bloody battle of Dieppe...I spent the grimmest 20 minutes of my life with one unit when a rain of German machine-gun fire wounded half the men in our boat and only a miracle saved us from **annihilation**."

—*Ross Munro reporting for The Canadian Press*

17

VICTORY AT STALINGRAD

Although weak from hunger, hollow-cheeked, and surrounded by ruined buildings, the people of Stalingrad threw a party last night. Why? The Battle of Stalingrad is finally over.

A Soviet soldier attacks a German position.

From the city

"I always knew we would win," said Oleg Karpov, who has been defending Stalingrad since July 1942. "Still, it'll be good to be able to walk down the street without worrying about German **snipers**. And I'm looking forward to having more to eat. It's as hard to find food here as it was in Leningrad!"

A turning point?

Is victory at Stalingrad a turning point in the war? One solider certainly thought so. Looking around at the ruined city, he made a grim promise: "In the end, Berlin will look worse."

Bütgenbach

Lunebach

Bül

Defeated German soldiers are marched through Stalingrad.

STALINGRAD: THE COST

Both sides have paid a high price in the Battle of Stalingrad. In total, roughly two million people have died in the fighting.

- Almost the whole city is now rubble. Few buildings are still standing.

- At times during the battle, the Germans controlled 90 per cent of the city, and the Russians held only the west bank of the Volga River.

- In November 1942, as the weather became cold, the Russians attacked. They surrounded the German 6th Army.

- Most Germans surrendered in February 1943. A few carried on fighting. They hid in cellars and **sewers**. By March, all had been killed or captured.

Gouvy

Burg-Reuland

Habscheid

Troisvierges

D-DAY!

DATELINE

7 June 1944

FRANCE

Aboard our landing craft, men crossed themselves, clutched lucky charms, or simply stared ahead. Then, suddenly, the boat lurched to a stop. The ramp at the front dropped, and the soldiers charged forward. The attempt to liberate France had begun.

Paratroops first in

The first Allied troops in France were British and U.S. paratroopers. They floated down through a sky full of German bullets just after midnight. Their job was to capture and hold key roads, bridges, and hills. This has stopped German **reinforcements** from reaching the landing sites on the coast.

Allied paratroopers rain down in northern France.

20

The view, as Allied soldiers wade ashore in Northern France

Beach landings

Just after dawn, the first Allied troops began to land on the beaches of France. British, Canadian, and American soldiers attacked five main landing sites. Despite coming under heavy fire as they waded ashore, the determined troops have successfully pushed the Germans back.

ESTABLISHING A BRIDGEHEAD

Allied soldiers are now battling to establish a **bridgehead** on the French coast. They need a secure area where more troops and supplies can safely be landed. Once this has happened, the Allies will break out of the bridgehead and begin the long fight toward Germany itself.

Trucks and men pour ashore to begin the fight.

IWO JIMA CAPTURED

Yesterday, the tiny Pacific island of Iwo Jima was at last captured. Small pockets of resistance remain as the Japanese fight to the death, but U.S. troops now control the island.

High cost of success

Many thousands of U.S. **Marines** have been killed or injured. The cost to the Japanese has been even higher. "They fought to the death," said one Marine. "I don't think any surrendered." Of over 20,000 Japanese soldiers, only 216 were captured alive.

U.S. Marines advance on Iwo Jima.

TOKYO BOUND

Superfortresses can now reach Japan

Iwo Jima's airstrips can now be used for bombing raids against Japan's cities. Bombers from Iwo Jima are expected to join the air raids on Tokyo very soon.

Bomber pilots are shown on their way to an air raid on Japan.

Fires smolder in an area of Tokyo destroyed by bombing.

RAIDS ON TOKYO

U.S. bombers have now destroyed a quarter of Tokyo, Japan's capital city. Experts suggest that 100,000 people have died, and 1.5 million have been made **homeless**.

While regretting any loss of civilian lives, we should remember three important points:

- Many civilians have died because of Japanese aggression.

- The raids have destroyed Japan's arms factories, wrecking their ability to fight on in the war.

- Ending the war will mean that the suffering of people in lands controlled by the Japanese will soon be over.

U.S. TROOPS CROSS RHINE

DATELINE

23 Mar 1945

GERMANY

By now, the news must have reached Hitler's bunker in Berlin. Yesterday, General Patton's Third Army crossed the Rhine River and entered the heartland of Germany.

U.S. troops step ashore after crossing the Rhine.

Nazi dream in tatters

Twelve days ago American soldiers entered Germany for the first time. The advance must have come as a further, terrible blow to Hitler. Now the **dictator** who once dreamed of enslaving Europe faces final defeat.

Germans on the run

"The Germans are on the run now," said American Corporal E. Robert Spiers of the 99th Infantry Division. "It's a race to see who gets to Berlin first—us or the Russians."

HORROR IN THE FOREST

DATELINE
6 Apr 1945
GERMANY

The people clinging to the wire fences are as thin as skeletons. Some cannot even stand up. Here and there, tears run down their cheeks—tears of joy. Freedom has come.

Place of death

This camp in the forest is named Bergen-Belsen, and it is a Nazi death camp. The prisoners are Jews, **Gypsies**, **homosexuals**, and others whom the Nazis despised. They had been sent there to work—and to die. Tens of thousands of people, maybe more, have died here.

A victim of the Bergen-Belsen Camp

A SURVIVOR'S TESTIMONY

"[There were] heaps and heaps of corpses stacked up. There was no way of burying them, getting rid of them. People died so fast and in such enormous quantities."

A mass grave in Bergen-Belsen

25

BERLIN TAKEN!

DATELINE
3 May 1945
GERMANY

After fierce fighting, Berlin has finally surrendered. The city has nearly been destroyed by the ferocious Russian attack.

The Soviet flag is raised above the Reichstag, after its capture by Russian troops.

A city in ruins

Few of Berlin's buildings are still standing. Everywhere there are piles of bricks—the ruins of houses and offices. People live mostly in cellars, the only rooms that are still intact.

Cleaning up Berlin

The smell of death is everywhere. Groups of civilians have been put to work hunting for bodies in the rubble. Hungry children dart around, looking for food. The Russian Army has started handing out food packages to the starving people.

Bütgenbach

Dateline: 3 May 1945

Lunebach   Büllingen

WORLD REJOICES AS HITLER DIES, BERLIN FALLS

Unable to bear the defeat of his armies, Hitler and his wife Eva killed themselves on 30 April 1945. Berlin surrendered soon afterwards.

"On the walls of Berlin's houses, we saw appeals, hurriedly scrawled in white paint: 'We shall stop the Red hordes at the walls of our Berlin.' Just try and stop them!"

—A Russian war correspondent describes the Soviet Army's entry into Berlin.

"Hitler? He got what he deserved, I'd say. It's just a shame it was the Russians, not our boys that got there first."

—Jeb Turner, a worker at the Lockheed aircraft factory in California, U.S.A.

"It won't make up for what happened in the Blitz, but I'm glad that man's dead."

—Beryl Tewkes, lining up outside a butcher's shop in London, England.

Allied soldiers advance through Berlin.

NAGASAKI HIT BY A-BOMB

DATELINE
10 Aug 1945
JAPAN

On August 6, the Japanese city of Hiroshima was destroyed by an atomic bomb. Yesterday, another atomic bomb was dropped on the city of Nagasaki, reducing it to rubble.

U.S. President approves bombings

Both of the devastating A-bomb attacks on Japan were approved by President Truman. He hopes that the terrible power of the bombs will bring the war to a quick end. So far, though, there has been no response from any of Japan's leaders.

Will Japan surrender?

The Allies demanded a Japanese surrender on 26 July. They said that non-surrender would result in, "the utter devastation of the Japanese homeland." Japan's leaders must now believe that this is true.

A mushroom cloud rises into the sky after the atomic explosion.

JAPAN SURRENDERS!

DATELINE
Sept 1945
JAPAN

Today, on the decks of the aircraft carrier USS Missouri, Japan formally surrendered. The surrender ended the war that has engulfed the world since 1939.

U.S. officers accept Japan's surrender.

Hirohito admits defeat

On 15 August, Japan's Emperor Hirohito told his people that Japan would surrender. To do otherwise, he said, would mean the Japanese people would be wiped out.

Cost of conflict

How many people have died in the war? As many as 60 million—two-thirds of them civilians. The lives of tens of millions more have been ruined. We can all agree with the shouts of the unnamed **GI** in Times Square. "Thank God it's over!"

Emperor Hirohito, Japan's head of state

GLOSSARY

Allies Group of countries who acted together during World War II, led by Great Britain, the USA, and the Soviet Union

annihilation Complete destruction

bridgehead Secure area where troops and supplies can land

bunker Underground stronghold

cellar Underground storage room

citizens People who are allowed to live in a country all their life

civilian Person who is not part of the military forces

conquest To take control of a place and the people that live there

dictator Person who rules people with force and does not listen to their views

evacuation Moving away from a place of danger

fiasco Complete failure

Filipino Person from the Philippines

ghettos Areas of cities where people persecuted by the Germans were forced to live

GI Nickname for American soldiers (short for either Government Issue or General Infantry)

Gypsies People of Romanie ancestry who travel from place to place

homeless People without a permanent place to live

homosexuals People who are attracted to people of their own sex

leave Holiday from military service

marines Soldiers in the navy

mobilization The preparation of armed forces for war

munitions Military supplies, including weapons

Nazi Member of the National Socialist German Workers' Party that ruled Germany from 1933 to 1945.

peninsula Area of land that sticks out into the sea or a lake

reinforcements Extra soldiers

resistance fighters People who fight against an invader, but are not part of the official armed forces

retreating Withdrawing or moving back from someone or something

rubble Broken brick left behind when a building is smashed to pieces

sewers Channels through which waste water can flow

siege Situation in which people are trapped inside a city because they are being attacked by an enemy

snipers Soldiers who lie hidden, waiting to shoot at enemies

Soviet Union A socialist state formed after the Russian Revolution of 1917 from most of the former Russian Empire

synagogues Places where Jewish people go to worship

Tommy Nickname for English soldiers

FURTHER INFORMATION

Web Sites

Visit the National World War II Museum in New Orleans at:
www.nationalww2museum.org

See photographs of the home front in the United States from World War II at:
www.archives.gov/research/ww2/photos/#home

Visit the Canadian War Museum in Ottawa at:
www.warmuseum.ca/swm/home/home

Read about the War at Home on this Web site from Virtual Museum Canada at:
www.virtualmuseum.ca/Exhibitions/Militaris/eng/home/home_i1.html

Find out more about World War II at the Imperial War Museum:
www.iwm.org.uk

Discover more about what life was like in Great Britain during World War II at:
www.bbc.co.uk/schools/primaryhistory/world_war2

Books

Eyewitness Books: World War II. Dorling Kindersley (2007).

World War II for Kids by Richard Panchyk.
Chicago Review Press (2002).

INDEX